# THE CLOUDS OF LUCCA

# THE CLOUDS OF LUCCA

*poems by*

## D. S. Butterworth

LOST HORSE PRESS
Sandpoint, Idaho

# ACKNOWLEDGEMENTS

*The Copperfield Review:* "Eleanora"

*ebraica Firenze:* "Alma Rosé, Violinist at Auschwitz"

*Eunoia Review:* "Remembering," "Vernazza"

*Florence Newspaper:* "Orphean," "Queen Thiedberge Escapes from Tour de le Reine," "The Wind of Umbria: Filippo Dreams from the Hilltop Towns," "In Tintoretto's Creation of the Animals," "In the Sala Capitolare," "Beyond Fiesole," "Sfumato," "Sistine," "Stendhalismo," "The Prisoner"

*Inscape:* "Reading a Poem I Don't Understand," "Writing a Poem I Don't Understand"

*Tidal Basin Review:* "Learning to Breathe"


Many thanks to Mark Alfino, Filippo Belacchi, Mark Bodamer, Pat Burke, Domenico Cannalire, Glen Colburn, Annie Dillard, Jim East, George Eklund, John Eliason, Mary Farrell, Christine Holbert, Gabriela Horvath, Chris Howell, Tod Marshall, Megan Metters, Mike Ramage, Tom Butterworth, and Jess Walter.

Cover Art by Mary Farrell. *Skin*, drypoint etching, woodcut, lithograph, 16" x 19 ¾"
Mary Farrell's art may be viewed at www.theartspiritgallery.com or www.davidsongalleries.com.

Author Photo by Amy Sinisterra.

Book & Cover Design: Christine Holbert.


FIRST EDITION

This and other Lost Horse Press titles may be viewed online at www.losthorsepress.org.


LIBRARY OF CONGRESS CATALOGING-IN-PUBLICATION DATA

Butterworth, Dan, 1955-
[Poems. Selections]
The Clouds of Lucca : poems / by D.S. Butterworth.—First edition.
    pages cm
ISBN 978-0-9911465-7-4 (alk. paper)
I. Title.
PS3602.U8926A6 2014
811'.6—dc23

                        2014026220

*for Beth, Bess, and Emma*

# CONTENTS

# THE CLOUDS OF LUCCA

The clouds of Lucca are the body of time mirrored
in mountains where woods are smoke drawing from fields.

Rain from the clouds of Lucca dreams of ochre and rust
walls, of streets worn to serenity from years of shoes

and meadowgrass drinking in a sky generous
with its memory of the sea, memory it feeds to Lucca

in the form of light to drain the grasses in streams
of sycamore and laurel. The clouds of Lucca dream

of climbing down human words on a ladder
of forgetting, of climbing from blank heights

down the history of stone and its cutting, of stone
and its assembling, of words and their easing

from the walls, and the void words shape with their
meaning, like rain and cloud, to loosen not the stones

but their inked filigree, not the words but the patina
of grains that are their shadow in the known world

where the clouds of Lucca and the rain of Lucca
dream as dust. For the clouds of Lucca dying

over Lucca enter into their dream of perfection
where all is draining from the everything there is,

and the clouds of Lucca and the rain wash us
whole as our human fires sleep themselves out.

## ii.

On the train from Lucca the Africans laugh
at the carbinieri who wouldn't believe their names,

laugh at Nigeria, its stream of presidents,
and at Italy, the same stream under a different name.

The loud music of their talk chases some from the car,
which they observe with musical laughter.

The laughter of the Nigerians comes in English and French,
Italian and whatever native dialects they use to understand

each other as they laugh at the Europe they have come to hate.
Because to send money home you need to work, and if you're ugly,

as they say they are, or if you're black, as they know they are,
you don't get work. You have to start with money to make money,

—*unless you're in Lagos*—they observe, before they laugh again
at the polizia who arrested them in Lucca and told them to move on.

*How far? Don't you like to say Africa begins at Rome?* The Nigerians
on the train from Lucca laugh, knowing they are and are not

a problem Italy needs to solve. Like the miraculous coda of a song
about solstice, like winter and summer themselves, these Africans

drift through, and though once philosophers or mathematicians,
now they must all be thieves, as if these are the only masks left

as the continents drift into one another with the tintinnabulations
of human collision, a sound like the laughter of the philosophers

from Lucca reeling in orbit, which is not unlike like the clouds above Lucca
in wind and rain, or rain from the clouds of Lucca draining the alleyways

of Florence, or like the polizia harrowing the bedsheets from Via Roma, hazing
Senegalesi from Repubblica to harass the purse merchants from the streets

like bigger dogs circling smaller dogs in patterns not unlike
the train from Lucca circling back again, or like fascism and anarchy

stepping in circles as they turn pages in history books,
or like the movement of the arm of the shop-owner as she paints

over the graffiti on the walls of Lucca even though the storm
will slip the paint with rain and the stones will run slogans in ink

through the streets of Lucca, and the clouds of Lucca will wear human shoes
onto the circling trains underneath the circling skies all described

in spirals of words that die into life somewhere beyond Lucca
where the marble-fired bones of the sea die into being, where mountains

wash into fragments and dream themselves again as cloud,
and laughter is a song wind sings drifting east of Lucca.

### iii.

The world calls to Lucca, and the world calls for clouds
to shed the light of forgetfulness on its broken ways.

Somewhere across waters a raptor dreams its ruin
through shattered stones and stirs coals with an iron

stick, as if a hotter kiln would fire harder dirt. America
dreams of clouds that will wash it of fate and time,

the same clouds that rain on Lucca, that rain on Africa,
rain that promises endings and beginnings, rain that cannot

read the language of walls, that does not recognize the voice
of the death it lives inside. Rivers call to the clouds of Lucca

for confetti of swallowflight, for swifts shrieking
in air's ecstasy, for thermals to drive the smoke

from our fires and drift rumor of tomorrow down the halls
of the spring and rinse memory to the bone. Oceans call the clouds

to wring drought from human thought, call for the clouds
of Lucca to extinguish the predatory sun, for clouds to die

as we die, and to rise as we die, for clouds under whose
enchantment the scavengers will whirlwind out, like the clouds

of Lucca that spin and drain the known world of meaning
so the rain can be felt for what it is, words heard for what they are:

water, and the sound of an animal in its turnings under clouds
where weightless the layered self unfolds to become the world.

## SISTINE

So who do you want to be at the secret
end of your pilgrimage,

the last place your weariness will teach
you, where gloom shades

expectation with understanding
as if the color of history

could fade? We have traveled
to the place our words have named

and found its shape bent
like a stick in water.

Beauty is the torque
of turning in time,

turning is the inertial
pull of change.

By the time we arrive
we are beaten down

to ghosts of ourselves,
the animal pulse

ready to howl
at whatever moon

will cross in orbit.
All roads led

the history of our lives
here, where we're reduced

to breathing as we gaze
at the story of the world

through the history of a man's hands.
Maybe we want to know

the same care has been shown to us,
our bodies wrapped in the paint

of creation to burn against the roof
of thought—even as the voices of the crowd

gather and rise, even as we waver into a sfumato
that is the human manner of moving through

history, the way people drain from the chapel,
the way smoke trails from the wick on its way out.

# VERNAZZA

*for Jess*

We've come to Vernazza to chase a god,
to hear a voice like fingers brushing silk.

We can choose our divinities here—sea, sun, and wind
in their easy omnipresence beat all thought down

to flakes of rust, light a powdered blindness
scaling the terraces above the orange trees

toward olive blades whittling the air. We can't imagine
who carved these paths and stairs, a net

to catch and hold the earth and ravel up the dark.
There should be a story about the sea climbing

these mountains for the love of stars, but broken
by a jealous sun fragmenting into towns like a self

divided into virtues musing their fledged origins.
Instead we have groves balanced on rifts of rock

where cliffs fall off the scales and oblivion swallows
us whole, like the train horn in the distance or the thrumming

waves shaping a continent to say we've caught
our venal god stealing the dinghies from the storm.

All paths wander this way through stone,
fretting the orchard terraces the same way ours does,

ancient steps shuttling us across ragged groves
our stories don't know how to describe,

the weary hours hauling disappointment overland
in sight of tides coiled against the end of journeying—

a weakness of flesh aslant the Mediterranean where we've
followed the ghost of ourselves to a hillside.

Everything we have ever been comes together
in this garden beneath a cottage: light and dark,

the white smudge of a harbor where the sea opens
out to all our days, orange and olive, goats

milling at the cistern, peppers drying on the sill,
the wind a necessity, feeding us the world.

We climb these paths not to haunt the lives
we would have lived, but the selves we were

and can become again, present to the earth
and to the moment even as we're passing through.

# A KAFUE WOMAN CROSSES THE RIVER

This emptiness is the derangement of history.
Across the floodplain of the Kafue a woman

and her two children thread tinder grass
to the ferry where canoe fishermen

pull their nets. Lack and plenty feed
their own hungers beaten to brass by sunlight

on miombo woodland. Three white storks
are the genius of the dambo, gliding

in emptiness like the memory of rain.
The crocodile muses over the flesh

of Brahmin cattle wading in waterweeds.
Emptiness is a leopard stalking in dreams'

darkness, the famine of spirits populating
nightcast land to rub its paste of phosphorescence

on our eyelids. Emptiness is death's generosity
in history, as in Africa, where presence is a current

through wire, time transfigured into a continent.
For emptiness is the void life rushes in to fill

the way the nets of the fishermen shimmer
with the fingers of the river to enter into the history

of the village, to enter into the gaze of highway traffic
passing through Mchinche, kapende-fish drying in the basket

on the head of a woman trailed by her two children
to the shade of the market stall where she sits

to watch the world burn and consume its madness
here, where the vein of the nation drains the continent

so wholly filled with another unrecognizable today.
Her child looks up and sees us for what we are.

## THE MORNING CUPS

The morning cups hold wine and snow,
they hold table top reflections of birds.

The morning cups have not dispelled the night's
delinquencies but only focus their gathering

weight. The morning cups hold the battle of Homs
and news of seven who died in car wrecks

on our city's streets these last twenty-four hours.
The morning cups are carrying the front shifting

in over the mountains from the Gulf of Alaska.
A famous person touched the morning cups once

before knowing ambition or disappointment.
The morning cups are full of dolorous confusion

and the hooves of three white horses. The morning cups
hold you and the morning cups hold me

where we look into our faces over the perfection
of the table's holding everything in place, and the morning

cups holding themselves as themselves, immaculately
what they are beyond word and story and meaning.

And when we are gone, they will find the morning
cups and remember us or not, but discover the open

sockets of the morning cups, as we do, before they
are glazed with the sky's dark waters.

## BEYOND FIESOLE

If beyond Fiesole our road rises through olive
dust to a quarry of cloud, do not tell
the cypress to dream of wind that is its only

awakening. If above Fiesole there is a road
along walls of *pietre serena* where sky is water
transfigured into light, do not tell the old women

frozen in the field that their branches bear
only emptiness. If the road beyond Fiesole
brings in the harvest from a blank sky,

do not tell the hillside that emptiness is Earth's only story.
Do not tell how the river teaches the valley what
mountains know about clouds, about dreams of dying

into the green dust of vineyards where
the olive women drown in their forgetting.
What is a road but the history of plans made

to get from here to there, from the gray dust
of the city to our dreamed home somewhere
above Fiesole? And now our roads are through rain,

the sweet fire of rain. Do not tell the trees
rain is the world's story whispered to itself,
a tale where to rise and fall rinses things of the marks

gravity scored on the passing. And if on the hill
toward Fiesole a cocoon on the olive loosens
a wing above the vineyards, tell flight the world wants

it so. Do not speak of time as conflagration
to the women of the olives, but of the blaze
that is the harvest of all things moving

into their beyond. Fate is the rage of voice
toward listening, the moth's throb above stony fields.
Do not tell the river home becomes a gesture

of a distant sea, how the flower is the seed's remembering,
eternity freedom's cell. Fiesole, blow us past your hills,
past the shrieking swifts, past learning and telling,
beyond ourselves and through the blue fluttering sleeve.

# STENDHALISMO

The chapel at San Croce saw him break down,
and it wasn't a disease caught from Galileo,

or from Buonarroti's bones radiating the weirdness
of death, or death's final void of guilt, or even

the certainties of stone, the stone's understanding
of eternity. Just that a writer doesn't know

when to leave a place, or that flesh and spring revolve
like the heart's valves in rhythm even as he writes

it so, or that those valves squeeze blood into the future
from the moment he first ached with the disappointment

of things passing. Beauty isn't the thing, but the doom
of living without it, knowing that it is there at all, dark

in the night, cold in the unopened hours, singing
in the unfolding flame of distance, burning in separation

where memory can only assemble a facsimile
and not the image itself still fresh and inviolable

under the force of gazes storming like solar flares
of some unearthly Pentecost the atmosphere of the chapel—

who among us wouldn't stumble the same way
if we beheld everything in the crush of a moment

held within a human hand, or impressed upon a wall
like the light of creation itself echoing down

the years' long corridor, just like Filippino's face smiling
beside a Madonna, or the eye of a beauty passed

in the last chapel, or a button gleaming from her immaculate shoe?

# SFUMATO

Etched in the mercury of this rain we're all sibylline—
prophetic of something beyond the edge of ourselves,

having traded much more than peace
for this destination, wondering what niche

or corner might hold our significance, what we are
or where, no longer caring who we are or why.

Is this Orvieto in the blue light of the night train
or rooms Raphael wrapped in damasked twilight?

In the window we only see ourselves—the world
has abandoned us to an unreeling earth,

the increate dream that was our becoming,
now a mask drooping from a fist, whether Perseus

or Jason, Judith or Persephone seems immaterial.
Like all myths ours is a taking and giving,

following the adventure toward the catastrophe
only to learn we already saved or damned ourselves

when the flower-skirted beggar dropped her stick
and we either stooped for it or didn't,

when we recognized her as she peered into our faces
and we abandoned the crucial moment. The mountains

of our story are crossed by roads through the heart
of ignorance, lessons lying in wait like rivers or beasts,

the same ones love lorn wanderers meet on pilgrimage
from their earlier lives to cure themselves of their past.

And that's the way night devours us now.
If all roads lead to Rome, so too do those that run

away, even headed north into the dark of Umbrian hills
where the tracks are paved with cockleshells and skulls,

where the promise of home is a last tricky distraction
before the train arrives and we become who we are

all over again, the way flame rekindles
the smoldering wick, the way dark spills into dark.

# WRITING A POEM I DON'T UNDERSTAND

You know how sometimes there's an image
rendered so perfectly you can see the sky

reflected in the ripe, polished berry of the bird's
eye, or there's a metaphor that has the world

falling away just like it does in sleep or a crisis
of love, the cattle entering the river and water lifting

the flesh off their bones in sweet redemption
from gravity, or the rain on the roof drums

like all eternity on the one grain time lent you
on yet another nasty day in early spring

or late fall, and the ember of tended fire circles
back to the eye of that waxwing and the weightless

flight of the cows swimming, and the connection
is effortless, words like the snake swallowing itself

up in a seamless loop of meaning so just and right
even our astonishment is easy? That's the kind of poem

this wants to be, but it reaches out with blunt fingers
cracked by cold, sore from abuses with rakes

and hammers, stuck drawers and windows, that box
of books in the attic, even the withering waters

of the sink. And though the bending light from down the hall
wants to shed this dark, it can't. The stupid ghost only

casts through the house a shudder that could be mistaken
for a passing truck or even an airliner rumbling overhead,

and all it manages are dim outlines and vague premonitions,
all it finds is a voice like the creaking hinge on a door

still resisting even as it opens. Maybe, too, that bird
or those cows sense a disturbance on the horizon,

a pick-up lumbering down a dirt road, a worrying
chainsaw or train cars' coupling boom at the edge

of town. But that would be the pixel storm straining
through the funnels of these hands as they stir

the waters of apparition. The inky corners fill
with dust as words I don't understand

swirl in the room's air of possibility, moved
by that door trying to shut before the meaning slips out.

# PRISONER

The prisoner's face is mere shadow, softer than stone
ought to be as it rises above his forearm bent

under the weight of the selfsame stone.

They say the bodies emerging from the marble
blocks meant for the Pope's tomb were the territories

he'd subdued, his arts pressed by the fierce

strain of impending death, an allegory
of the artist in the chains of duty, or even Ficino's

favorite story about the soul trapped in the body.

I've never been in prison yet still I feel the crush
of freedom lost, the burden of care, labor spilled

upon labor, time precious as blood, rendered

in the cruciform of words on a page forever unread.
So. The prisoners are exactly what they are: no

misinterpretation from a bad translation,

no trick of perspective rising above an enormous
hand, not even a theory worked out in the hardest

earth, but figures carved in rock cut from a mountain

to give a human shape to the final darknesses. This I know.
It's the light around them, and the air that kindles

any possibility of meaning

where stone becomes as soft as flesh
and lifts a lifeless face into our lives as if to ask

what we are and why, and how we rise beyond
our selfsame flesh to bear the weight of our lives.

# IN THE SALA CAPITOLARE

The French woman in the Sala Capitolare
draws the eyes of the apostles from Fra Angelico's

*Crucifixion and Saints*, the *memento mori*, too,
grins at her from the frescoed wall like desire

incarnated as a demon calavera. Only flesh
can conjure such astonishment. They look away

from the scandal of their Lord's death, the other
consequence of incarnation, on his sad wooden bed.

The neckline of her chemise and thin strap
across her ankle bone remind us how skin

always comes by its promises easily, and as easily
casts away its companion dress, how figure and cloth

wed only to undo the mystery of their consummation.
Ah, the mind is a den of thieves—our quiet that looks

so much like piety is anything but. The wet walls
of the fresco dried ages ago, and now the afterthought

of that meditation fixes the stoic and disbelieving faces
of ancient men on her lovely earring, on the hair curled

around her ear, the bracelet holding her wrist. Shell-
shocked, the saints have gained their first epiphany—

the way a body fills its clothing teaches them the mistake
of holiness, denying rather than accepting, like Job's friends

insisting he must have sinned only to be condemned
by the voice from the whirlwind, the same way her body's

miracle of will and motion condemns them to know
that they wear a flesh their God would die for. She turns to her

companion with a smile in front of the fresco over-restored
into something that will pass for a brilliant painting

and the chapter room trembles as the image of her face
ignites into flame that burns through flesh like grace.

# FILIPPO DREAMS BEYOND THE HILLTOP TOWNS

## i

From the piazza we will clouds into bloom
the way you must hope for stone itself to break open

into the future, like fragments of bread offered
against the deepest thirst.

Ancient shrieking birds cry over the town.
The town—an old man hauling

his bones in the basket of the seasons.
Still he's convinced he is young, an ancient deception

by which everything gathers into an artifice of stone,
the porphyry of tombs, marble temples,

dilapidations of colonnade where the wasted years
gather shades of desire to drown all in memory.

These hill towns are images of their quarries in negative
against the photographic plate of the sky,

their silver gelatin fixed against a blue hole
where possibility left a scar. Even quarries fill with water.

And though there is no forgiving the past,
maybe the past will forgive us this fate of stone.

Can vineyards teach us to move over earth toward fullness?
And, too, the olives, old women who tell us youth is nothing

as they choke on the ragged dirt of weeds—can their revolvings
free desire from the axle of seasons,

or must weeping be axiomatic? Mud dries after rain
on the same dull road where stone strives with stone

to achieve these heights over the same winefields
and stone, and groves weave the same bone baskets.

If only a town were a sleeve to be pulled inside out
through the exfoliation of itself. If only these blossoms

were real flowerings instead of rain thrown against walls
to gather still more dust.


## ii.

Voices gather at the doors of cafés,—voices rise from stone
like flames of water above the hard surface of the town

as if there were something to believe, not the way a god
is believed or the way a god rises from stone,

but the way water gathers to irrigate the dream
of a body moving to music unimaginable.

Can anything happen in a town made of stone—
love or hunger or words—to meet those voices

at the café? And the old man, can anything come
from his desire? Is all desire the lust of old men

for what they once held, and is all holding
possession without knowledge of time,

the way stone holds water or hilltown streets wind?
Excitement runs through the village as if something

were suddenly possible, some wonderful machine
or news from the far edge of civilization. Women

circle the flame of the photographer's camera—it is
the only way they see themselves before dissolving

into gloom, and men grab cameras so the women
will see them before they grow old. Magazines teach

how they might live, but what they learn of love
and desire are rediscoveries. Yet still the voices

rise in praise of motion, images of impossible
moments at the edge of what's real, and for an instant

it seems the future is something other than a place
where you are an old man carrying your basket,

where even the dogs tell you there are only hungers
and satisfactions that loosen our vacancies,

that the glorious past we yearn for tumbles in olivelight
where the moon howls against a vineyard wall.

### iii.

A word falls against a body like a moth's wing.
The motions that are the shadow of its meaning

cut or break, but a word has no conception
of the movement following in its wake.

Kings and presidents, queens and duchesses
find gods in words and build empires

with wind and shadows of blood, but wind
makes no promises as it moves over the earth,

remembering only the hot and cold that pushed it
while the holy breed monsters to fill the future.

In the cities words move like wind to fill the space
around hunger. Airless words die like dust on rock.

Towns scatter words to the wind through stone canyons,
the urgent careless ephemera of thorns, desire dying

against the walls like wind, before the symbolic,
when everything was what it was.

## iv.

Wind moves through Umbria like birdsong.
Clouds bloom, burn, then blow out in wind.

The wind of Umbria polishes buds of olive in pearl
clusters held in the hands of women turning to dust.

Trees blaze with birdsong and wind drains the towns
of light. Sound is a web wind lays over the fields.

Rosemary is a child of wind, lavender the wind's indecision.
Yellow birds glitter in the trees like wind. Moving through

the leaves, wind tells us nothing, just like the voices of dogs
from the vineyard. Like the voices of the branches swaying,

the wind can say nothing, empty and invisible,
only signifying through the things it moves. Like words,

which tell us nothing but their sounds and the time marked
in their uttering, wind dips like swallows above a pool

or traces lines of graffiti defacing a monument
to describe another hunger, an urge inscribed

in vacancy like the voices of dogs
from the vineyard, like the motion of shadows

cast onto the world. The wind from the hills reveals
itself through the motions of many centuries, the movements

of the shadows that traced its passing over Umbria, itself a wind,
itself a revelation telling us nothing but its sounds and shadows

blowing through the hot moments of our being. Ah Filippo—
all towns are made of stone, even glass and steel ones.

At the ends of the earth Odysseus found only a rock
rising in the shape of a mountain and even the sea

became dirt tilled with a winnowing oar. The brilliant
moon too, is stone. But go. We travel these distances to see

how far we can run when empires crumble. All towns are hives
burning with a faith there's something more than field

and distance, voice and image. Find a new stream of verbs
for old love, follow borrowed light's bloom under clouds

to the ends of your earth where epiphany is configured
as a new kind of town where the streets you knew died

ages ago, where stone dissolves into the ruddy air
of the now and a future gathers from the dust of then.

# FROM THE INTERIOR

## i.

Wind lights a wick of masamba from this howling sun.
Jackals range in the million-year-old shade

of a termite hill. Our names have no meaning.
Words die, tree by tree, soil breathes copper

smoke, tinkers and weavers build meadowgrass
towers. The predations build their strength to destroy

the confusion of men. The talk of men covers the earth.
Reason and fear lay out their net of hornets

to explore the aptitudes. Clouds plot the desolation
of huts. Cattle ranchers burn lweo grass

to assemble a compound out of smoke. Kudu
read the stars to antelope. Leopards bless

the hungry children. Welcome to the thralldom
of appetite—a miombo woodland path.

The road we left, too, was madness.

## ii.

Witchdoctors wear shoes and dishes on their heads.
When the sky collapses they call it nightfall.

Machines plough the highway in dark velvet.
Morning cracks open from an ember like an egg.

Poison in the soil leeched from bones of colonists.
God is blind: half fire, half water, extinguishing

himself with the fuel of his being. Ash rains
from an exploding field. All roads lead to Congo

where they derange the order of things one green
parrot at a time and smuggle the hours over the border

into tomorrow. Wash us with the dirt of home,
wash us with the smoke of age, wash us with

the flame of our original place.

## iii.

When snakes fight follow them through memory.
The world is a coiled line that draws the smoke of winter

into the shape of thought. The cobra weaves adder-light
and the black mamba drinks in the cobra's shadow.

We have become the tree and the orchid in the tree.
We have become the medicine the snake consumes

to heal the wound that, rising from the earth, is our
separation from earth. When the snake returns

to the lifeless ribbon of the adversary, follow, and if it spits,
as grandmothers say, the dead will rise again.

And so with us. Nothing that lives completely dies.
Nothing born of the soil is denied returning.

The road from Lusaka flares over the brindled earth
like a snake wound around a fist, the same fist that

flung the stars fresh as the honey wind grass breathes
over the face of the deep. Night is free from cruelty, accepts

predation in a silence spoken as darkness. Copper trucks
prowl the highway, ghosts without eyes.

The thorn in the tree branch? Witch hid it for the enemy.
Make fire from this wood to ruin friendship.

Build a house from this wood to fix your doom.
The ordeal tree makes red water—drink and die of innocence

or be healed by guilt. If we have not forgotten
them, ancestors will provide rain. When we pass

the field the white stork will lift us into her mind.
The rainbow lives in the anthill. Sitondo directs rain

over the barren with his fly switch. Charm-horn and snakeskin
outwit the incantations of the last born to drift rain

from the elders over the village. Witches ride the whirlwind
scattering amber to burn the huts of the wicked.

Images of Bantu dream crack underfoot like potshards,
the chief's nightmare pours illumination on crocodiles

haunting cattle on the river.


### iv.

The spirits of the trees are what earth has borne
from the long quiet. According to prophecy, they walked

to the gates of paradise but remained inside
to study the angel's sword of flame,

a vision of steel and machine,
and shunned the fall into having.

They remain in the trees far above the world of things.
Paradise is a field in the mind of the chimpanzees,

a forest where berries ripen in sun and the chimpanzees
build nests in masamba branches in the guise of spirits.

At the edge of language we stare at each other
to mourn what we both have lost.

Paradise is the mind of sunlight and wind
before metaphor, where words don't have other words

to describe them, the mind before we became metaphors
for each other, the ape that has, the ape that hasn't.

From the bliss of consciousness they are
the raw blood of earth and do not enter

a heaven where they already dwell
with nothing to let go of beside the outrage of flesh

as they watch the apes of things breathe diesel
from mouths that have not yet learned how not to want.

## LOST IN VENICE

Inside the rooms of San Toma
heat works on the body

the way guilt filters through memory
and water rises through stone.

Senegalese bundle faux Prada bags in sacks like coal;
pigeons test the evening with necks of Ubangis,

flaring like the gaze of an angry Doge.
Come. Drink at the fountain. Lift the smoke

from your cigarette like the white garments
on the clothesline baffled by a breeze up the canal.

Doorways dream of submergings
inconsequential as whatever conquest

and defeat built this maze
between San Marco and San Frari.

The four horses of St. Marks configure
this ordinary, surfaces scored to reduce

the glare, their copper alloy hosting
a gilt mercury that is their flesh. Only centuries

of saints enmeshed in stone will tell
you you're lost in Venice,

floodwaters rising toward those lights
that sink toward the canal in your heart

where a face gleams through darkness
rare as a Bellini maiden, a glance

that tells you *this is it,* this is finally where you are—
where you don't speak the language,

where maps are useless, where everyone is mad,
at home in the actual precisely because you don't belong.

# ARRIVING

*after the paintings of Bonnard*

When you arrive there will be fruit in a bowl
on a table, and it will be composed of pure

tones of rain and orchard. And there will be
a figure in a room and the room will have a name,

and the figure. There will be understandings
within the interior as if the arrangement of objects

was designed by the history of intent transacted
in those spaces, as of course it was. And your arrival

will be marked by brushstrokes of light along
the tablecloth, crimson and indigo rubbing the curve

of illumination bending around a corner, the bowl
and plate, a window with poplars along a river

like torches of keening ochre, on the sill a lilac
branch in a glass. And when you arrive, the presence

of things will have the quality of snow or leaves
or cottonwood cotton in a wind you will recognize

as the fragrance of the place, and the time in which you
find it, and you will know the room has found you

the same way, as if with its own gaze, as if its presence
and being are a body, yours or someone else's, awakening

to what is, stirring to breathe beyond the self
and other, the arrival of all the dappled colors we've become.

# GATHERING

As we drove to apple picking the mountain
flashed between the trees along the highway.

We watched wrestled wheelbarrows bounce
down rutted lanes of grass and dirt, already

feeling our own weariness build into impatience
though our only labor was to walk and breathe

and find those emptier corridors where branches
cantilevered into archways. Our visit to the orchard

was so brief not one crystalline pip of apple flesh
ripened as we passed across the day's photographic

plate. But even this was too much, brushing against
the lean, hardened curve of time, the season's slow

sweet skin, sunlight and air tumbling into the shuttered
rooms of our skulls, dizzying. We gathered only what

we could hold, the road back an unfurling ribbon rushing
us home to nap, taut little globes spinning in our hands.

# ORPHEAN

Colored wheels of whirligigs rise
against Repubblica's arch

where the soprano sings *Torna A Sorrento*
and the jangling of hammer

dulcimer from the gypsy jazz
band joins the streetsweeper

to send a roar against the buildings
as the carousel lights revolve

horses around the inner ear of the piazza.
As the waiter works the bicycle chain

back on the spindle for the *bella donna*
and the Carbinieri harass Senegalesi street merchants,

it's the fire dancer who answers the question
who we are and where, or why we are

and what it matters: spume of dust
flaming out in the ghost of the old ghetto's

shadow. But only down Via Roma
will the conditions of our mortality

become clear, where the ciotoli artist
measures the forehead of a goddess

in centimeters, the distance from eye
to ear rubbed into pavement stone

where we are the grains of a crayon smear,
the chalk dust of our being

peeled like the flesh of sycamores,
ribbons blown beyond the piazza—

*find love, find love* spore fluff offers
in dry drizzle-fall from the canopy,

fawn umbrellas parachuting like snow
over Piazza Massimo D'Azeglio

and colors of confetti along Via Della Colonna
fade to the same dun as, glancing back,

Eurydice entered falling into Orpheus's memory
a second time, the way Florence does now,

the old palazzo rising against a bowl
of terra cotta, Miniato swimming like Jupiter's

moon through Galileo's telescope,
the tides of the city rushing past the homeless

man whose rant, brittle as broken wine,
echoes in the loggia

where some vain Medici rides a bronze horse
against the uncertain composition of the sky.

# OFF WELLFLEET

and you turned, like a god in exile,
out of your wide primeval element,
delivered to the mercy of time

*Stanley Kunitz: "The Wellfleet Whale"*

## i.

Off Wellfleet a whale slips through the dream of water
an unfathomable shape multiplying into images of selves

suspended and amniotic within the earth like stacked dishes,
the nerve of our imagining a marionette's string

coiled through vertebrae to the stars. The whale's drift sweeps
the planet in its glacial riptide of sea to swallow down the galaxy.

The Wellfleet whale teaches the past to the future, future
to ancient seasons that blow through the body's memory

troweling the history of a hand against the mind that is
the hand's cloud of motion, the hand's albido, that glow

of moondust whose shadow of emptiness is the total
of lived lives dwindling in the memory of the hand.

The Wellfleet whale was in the mind before the eye, as it is now
swimming in the blankness or rising to the surface

to conform to the mind's taming; the whale swims seas
that rise to final skies, the farthest tidings of the world.

The Wellfleet whale is the world's body, each sleeping head
a door open to the mind of the world that holds the whale like

a sound moving through depths. The Wellfleet whale tells
us world and mind are one, plied polarities, the play of difference

othering down the throat of the same body, where rose and fire,
the dying children, weir and channel stone at the chamfered edge

of town are the whale drifting arteries into the real in cathedral
patterns. Surf hammers plaster away from the body of the world

which is the swimming whale: fresco, terracotta, the stress-bearing
armature of rooms, hammer-beam roof and trefoil arch,

exfoliations of the same current, all shriveled into the beached nothing
of this morning. Wood worn to splinters offers a turnbuckle shape

to the mind of the whale that raises the tide, a hinge, an oarlock
collar turning to the mind of the whale and to the mind of a woman

floating unimaginably upon each other's seas like gods of other worlds,
each a vastness of particularity vaulted into water, each a consciousness

certain of something asserting the nothing that is all there is.
But the Wellfleet whale describes the chisel's end of it, the polished

surface where the sun burnishes the world in the eye. The whale is all
that can be made with words, it is the novel and the poem,

it is the looming shade of imagination moving in its own life
but not so wholly realized its naming is complete. The Wellfleet whale

navigates deep and shallow waters, and like the mind that is water,
hollows out itself with itself.

## ii.

The woman inside the house is mad with the intelligence of the world.
Her voice builds the whale rib by rib even as it slakes memory with sand.

Memory is the debt she owes for seeing things as they are,
unmediated by the words which form the shoreline on which the day

and all its ravelings shallow and beach. In the whale range the particulars
from a dying nebula's hydrogen shells fusing into the planetary allotropes

between Arcturus and the house on the beach— where ancient
light bathes cells in atmospheres of time and place, and locks

its shed photons in the lobed valves of the sea. Memory is her desire
reflecting back to flung dark the image of an iris. The whale is the bow drill

ocean leathers to spark fire, the jawbone of an ass broken by antler hammers
on a future foretold by auguries of bird ash and electron, keelbone steering

offshore. The whale's breath defines the tide, dilations of claw and riffler
pumiced down with air's chisel and mallet and honed by a bullnose sun.

Eternity has gathered for the woman in the house to hold in her mind.
The whale that is the body of the world is the woman and it is her mind.

In the woman's mind words stain the unfathomable waters with ink,
pixels configuring what we can know of naming, predation's

anchor fixing the everyday to the deeps, the edge of voice crazing
as the whale weighs off Indian Neck. Fire scours the armature as the bronze

light floods the casting of wax. The world and the whale rush
in to burn the socket where once the forms held fast, her mind kindled

and doused but whole, like light in water, water's dense vacancy. So words
are wind and light themselves: pure quavers from the buoy's flared bell.

So the woman and the whale configure one another as lures to catch daylight:
eye to hook, head and ribbing to tail, shank and barb bent against the throat

of permanence, the barrel swivel of change angling up through currents, tides,
weathers, hours, drags, releases, frames, forges— a swimming up inside her,

a knowing that is a scumble at the edge of a continent. The whale is intelligence
and the intelligible upwelling from the neap of abyssal waters. The whale

is nation and history rendered as moths of foam baffled on the waves.

### iii.

And now the beached whale, an image stranded within memory, pauses
to breathe and die under its own weight. A neighbor falls mowing grass

as earth seizes his heart, a plane shudders through mountain updraft,
the lucky penny gleams against the sidewalk, mantis thorax flutters

through wildrose, headlights flare across the night wall of the girl's room,
and there's a change in the air—the smell of the timeless entering into time.

As waters fill Wellfleet Harbor, Lieutenant Island and Indian Neck assume
the same feral order as the hills beyond Roanoke or tides off Wisteria Island

or where eternity runs through Blackfish Creek to fill its thirst for marshgrass
and feral ooze, fingers the mud of Drummer Cove, and sweeps over a million

fiddling crabs. The Wellfleet whale has drained into shallows the way we follow
any wake to nothingness, to the release from the fever of its burning.

The whale is the thigh bone of the ram heaved over the altar of the continent
into the eyes of the world, a blown rose.

## iv.

Rimless, leeward winds are the weather of forgetting.
She withers under the hood December draws over June. So many

are undone by this crazy singing. Wintry light flares across the rooms
of the house, walls blank pages where words once told her story.

The house, too, has become a conjurer's trick, windows wide, screen-cells
honey-combed with brine, curtains taking the shapes of young bodies,

Eurydicean, burnt, and tangled. Nothing from something, tablecloth
and cupboard doors fluttering derangement, sand blown through rooms

of moondust and pollen. An emptying out, hammock cord squeaking under
absent weight, photographs curling. Gulfstream aslant a Canary breeze

and always the mad singing of daughters and fathers and husbands and wives,
of love that will not perish, that permeates like moisture the grains of salt

in the shaker, that shakes the house like the mad emptiness of sirens
blowing in the desolations. An amanuensis recites inscribed lines

with the pitiless intensity of sunlight, mistakes his beating heart
for the dirge of seasons. And now she hears the scientist bicker

with the priestess, the mother with the demimonde, shrew with martyr,
voices rising within her like an actor's dream, and the Dickensian gentleman

loses a wager with the shriveled pensioner and the hopes of the cottagers
are dashed, the drama splintering into the prayer-wheel's copper script,

the cocoon of a cecropia moth, skull of mistle thrush, Devonian
trilobite, garnet-mica schist, Antarctic meteorite—

all flicker through the cave of the house in that same wind
that blows through the mind, filaments raveled from the wholecloth

sail that is the house, the crumbling spiral of the familiar in the teeth
of the on-coming tide, splinters of the known world cast off like photons

from the incandescence of the whale, smashed electron shells shedding
like rain drops from broken glass the pigments of a butterfly's forewing,

fragments of the last moments of the whale's being, the last exhaled
spume and wrack of the mind's created world, there, on the sandbar

half way to Indian Neck, under a gray sky of calling birds,
the urgent indifference of the elements swallowing everything up.

**v.**

Maybe the whale felt the waves off Nauset, heard the ocean
strum the other shore, its currents plunging sand through the thin

hand of the cape, a wrist worn to paper. Maybe it read the watermark
on the land's meniscus and tried to break open that eelgrass palimpsest,

the glow of meaning shining through from the Atlantic like light
through the finest porcelain. Memory undoes itself this way,

lunging into the now, water through a screen, image and thought
shell scraps enmeshed in nerves' net, the current rushing

away from itself to whatever depth runs from the other side,
the gravity of the wider home Socrates sensed when dumb

he paused by the cistern gate rapt with the mute siftings,
Helen's surmise as channel waters rose with offshore wind,

Queequeg's fatal tattoo inscribed as a body on the skin of a wave,
scrimshaw of smoke from the captain's tossed pipe on a wooden wheel,

Lear's muttering dumbness or the train conductor's blind piloting—
memory's ossuary is a snow globe, silent rattling in a shook bag,

sweet water's scent drifting from Barbados and the mind's
far islands that steal us back, like the whale, beaching on Indian Neck,

driving to that home against which Death is small porridge in the wake
of the heaviest weighing, a sackful of pixel teeth crashing when the lights

go out. Maybe it simply wanted the other side. If the life of the whale,
like the life of the mind, by the presence of its body on the sand

conjures the mind's idea of the thing that stands behind it, the ghostly
assertion of the well from which the whale and the words spring,

then that too is undone with the whale's flesh, the incarceration
of memory in flesh, the demarcation of absence and presence

together in one tide, the line between figure and ground, shore and sea,
reversed on the plate of a photogravure, filaments of copper

sprayed out like burrs of beach grass or applause scattering through the hall
when the song is over, and the whale and the thought are the song

which only lives through the dying of itself giving way to the next note,
moments strung like bicuspids around the neck of the photographed aboriginal

in a magazine of pages closed to the world on a shelf of shelves in a room
of rooms. Maybe the whale sought the other side the way we pull out her words

like relics from the body of the saint miraculously preserved in death
without diminishment, each sentence a trace of a Magdalene paraded through

ancient streets of the brain by our desire to reach the far shore through this one,
the whale and the mind merest filaments on the beach time litters

with stories as it gathers June light above us through the racing leaves. Fool
brain, fool whale, running your own stream to earth's gravel-bedded oblivion.

## vi.

There is the whale, and there's the woman, and the woman
holds the whale as the whale holds the sum of existence

by moving through it. They do and do not know each other
in the amniotic sea that is time's manifestation of itself

rushing into itself. But they know as witness, stalker,
as the whale sees by feeling the powers that thrum its body

hurrying it to its end. Oblivion resolves into the particularity
of house and beach, the nest of nerves and gaps the synapses leap.

And so the whale enters into mindlessness, the ocean it wears
like a tunic of coal, the shore it plumbs like a sword.

As they become each other the woman and whale die the same way
and within each other's gaze in the air above Indian Neck. And time

considers their meeting, osprey and the harassing blackbird
of the fussing mind, or osprey and caught fire—the scale-flash

of herring in the clutch, or whirling synchronicity of a bait ball
and scaring flock beneath and above the separations.

In the rush into the other, house and shore are shuttle and loom,
where the book ends at the blood's inscribing.

In the world that describes the world, the Wellfleet whale
is the word behind the word, the ancient story of earth

resting on turtles resting on turtles all the way down
the ruined pillars of the cathedral that is existence

in the ruined mind of the woman in the house, in all broken
minds, the only minds there are.

For Iphigenia, Homer, Helen, God—they are the whale as spoken word
against writing, the secret sacred meaning before the book,

and the whale is the book of pages thin as Cape Cod's
curled arm, testament of the lone survivor living

to tell the tale to the wedding guest, the ghostly consumed
interlocked words in sentences, sentences in lines,

limpet encrusted limestone shelves shingling the continent
where things break down into fragments of themselves,

the complete and final dismantling. Is this the return to the vacancy
behind the sign, the final effacement of word, body, and being

blossoming into the incomprehensible and pre-comprehensible
a-transcendent, the void blank empty where metaphor is broken,

presence suspended, systems of difference upended? House and whale,
the woman's body and the shore, the bric-a-brac of the cupboards

are inhabited by wind off Wellfleet, but the gargantuan brain
and ribs have foundered in the dog calm of that unmasked wind

and become the traces that are what they are, utter, without
meaning, dead fireless grains, unsusceptible to the mind's rendering,

beneath alphabet, beneath choral ode, beached at the broad imponderable,
the flat dimensionless void where height and depth,

the saturations of meaning and molds of categories are not,
uncreated, waste, the one singularity, where the verb to be

dissolves into the wild atoms of the random, the deepest deep,
unnamed, before the drama of death, before stage, before page,

the unfathomable shapelessness before possibility, the lumbering
vastness, drear but wicking cocoon of stars.

# vii.

But blank, the mind of the woman ranges the same shore
the whale seeks for dying. It is the woman's manner of life,

and so the way she dies, casting neurons against the pages
like spendthrift seed on salt shore. Her pages burn

even as she renders anarchy to the self's perfection,
but knows that behind the sweetness and light rage

subterranean flames, shown on the manuscript pages
as a frying pan, a figure-study dividing the face into quarters,

the crow and appaloosa fading into cloud forms dappling
creek-edge like the nosing arrowhead of the weasel

plumbing for the eagle's heart. First things merge with last,
protagonists and antagonists shape-shifting into one

another. And now it's the families inscribed in books
that melt into each other, first wives, second best beds,

the cat paw-printing rose petal tattoos on your skin,
the betrayal of daughters, houses whirl-winding far

into and beyond the adopted familiarity. The mind
of the woman reads page after page and follows the arc

of the story as if it were the crimson thread through a needle
made of bone, wrapped with vervet hair worming its way

to the heart. But each page introduces a new character,
each character having been immolated with the turning page,

and the flutter of moth wings as the book unfolds itself
has the rush of inevitability, and words build, inked filaments

and sculpted vacancies as the words become seconds, minutes,
hours, days, weeks, months, seasons, years, generations,

neighborhoods the mind has spun through in a galaxy of instances
on the way to the last room in the last house, the last current in the last sea,

the last thin shore opposite Nauset where Indian Neck names
other passings, the last inevitable sailing which is the passing of all.

## viii.

Dismantling resolves the parts of the thing into everything it is not.
Letters scatter to the margin where the text posits itself

as other, and the blanknesses fall into the center, as if here,
the one singularity of meaning resides as a simulacrum of meaning.

The world consumes itself in the slow fires of predation.
The mind consumes itself with words. The mind and the world

are one and the same, the fatal game of their desiring life and death.
And in this arena mind wants its one thing, simple

as the being of the whale in its sea, and it wants its one simple thing
to be a word, for the mind is words the way the whale is an anthology

of cells, a novel of sentences, the way the sea is hydrogen and oxygen
folded into molecules with salt and diatoms and the cells of the whale,

and words are the letters that compose the one word that sums up all
and the simplicity of words and the directness of words is their spelling

out the only thing there is, the thin shore between the sea and the nothing
that holds the sea and to which the sea rises in its eternal becoming the one

singularity, infinitely dense, the vortex that pulls the spinning mind,
the void cavern of sunless seas where uttered words dissolve.

And that is what the woman sees when she places the bowl on the table,
and the curtains flutter, and the spoon rings. Things resolved to their pure

image and form, their absolute connectedness and location, pure relations
of light and window, doorjamb and floorboard, unmediated presence,

uninscribed, unremembered, uninterpreted,
situated in the field of being, seen there the way

a painting sees abstractly, dismantled into movements
of color and a stasis of shapes until the spiral of whelk

becomes it all and the whale and the woman and the house
and Indian Neck are the translucent sheen on its inner whorl.

## ix.

She sees the whale swim not in blankness but in being.
Illusions of presence on a page, the sleight of hand

that lifts the whale into the mind from the pixel sack
of ocean, the inked filigree is the firm, holy destination

of molecule's push toward cell, the electric journey
toward reason, time's galactic hurl pointless and pointed,

a pilgrimage of dust from exosphere to vernal tropes
of flesh and dirt and word, and the fatal magic of meaning.

The window screen glows with bacterial scum, shudders
in the wind that is presence as she balances the whale

on the blade of awareness teetering to awareness of awareness,
entry into the whale's image in her living mind. And this

is where the wind is craziest, in this doubling that blooms
out from the fed and feeding mind, in this krill of thought

that stirs the hive and races through the baleen of its hungers.


X.


The dismantling: for the woman it is a question of tools.
Because the whale, like the thing that is given in consciousness,

is always already flayed and flensed—in the mind its rendering
analyzes down to details, and the flesh it wore as it wore the ocean

has evaporated into the cells of the fish, fowl, and fleet,
into the lamps and perfumes and lotions and factories

buckled, shocked, and shuddered into the ocean and the feeding
mind interpreting and resolving all to nothingness in the feral digestion

that is the way the world has of consuming itself. Riffler,
gouge, hammer, hone, chisel, rasp, burnisher, saw,

needle, fid, marlinspike, lug, pin, martingale, spit,
staple, shackle, grip, mallet, hook, lanyard, fiddle block,

drill, claw, ferrule, pestle, brush, nib, reed, scribe, rocker,
roulette, scorper, lens—each the name of a petty god

for whom we feed at the hearth our little fires. The whale requires
all, and the staining, corrosive flames of words lick

flesh from flesh, worry the skeleton from itself,
analyze bones into constellations, organs into meanings,

rib, skull, and jaw into doorjamb, threshold, footstool,
and myth to compose a Babylon and dismantle Marduk's

mat of rushes and Oceanus's lineage, the stab of Raven's beak
to fix water serpents in the deep.

Let us go down to the shore of our imagination,
to that place that is our always returning

and help the woman tell the story of the world
and its intelligence, its incessant kindling against the blankness

of Zephyr's blessing at Psyche's birth, the apparition of an angel,
the draping of figures without faces and hands,

the texture of the painted wall, the detail of the painted line
we trace to find ourselves. What is this self, this now,

presence, and consciousness, but the world, but the sign
flowing through the mind's construction of place and time,

and what is the mind but the actuality of the whale on the beach,
of the woman in the house, the fluke of wind, the unhinged

transcendent that flesh and place, word and page, play out
in nothing more or less than the drama of salt sea rising

and falling, nothing more or less than the heart's already
beating, the throbbing of the bird and its frantic wings?

### xi.

As we converge on the beach, the Wellfleet whale rises
into disenchantment. We live on the rim of that beach:

in dead trees and fired clay, clothed in dead hair and plants, eating dead
flesh, we take the whale into the mind of our body.

Scavenged debris gather where the wind dies. We live by consuming
until finally the mind turns to itself. As we stand on the beach

to behold the whale, our hands are stained with oil from the drill
and wrench, the rusted bolt on the handle of the saw rubbed red

onto the skin, sawdust blown into our eyes as we weigh
the chevron bones sunlight built. To undo this spell

of sacrum, scapula, metacarpal, we swarm the whale
to become its decomposition and convert it to our uses

in the rush nothingness makes into and from itself.
Even in our immaculate rinsing we taint the rift,

the drag-sail billows against the skids as if we were stone
fingers in glacial motion in the face of a storm.

As we dismember the whale, the sands of Wellfleet swallow
us whole, and we are smothered by the shifting surfaces of things,

Tarshish and Nineveh, promise and doom, slogging in the belly
of eternity, sinking into time and freezing there, invisible.

In this disintegration the human variables are resolved—
the advance of dismantled mountains sweeps house, woman,

whale, the blowing curtains and all intelligibility away.
Novel and poem are reduced in this burial,

thousands of pages, the torrent of words whittled down
to the one final salient of wind, vessels carrying vessels

into metaphor's further shore where the mind is vanquished
between kellick and astrolabe, tree and page, beach sand

and monitor screen, gaze and photon, whale and woman,
as strand and house become the same one articulated thing

howling through the world.

# xii.

And just like that, off Wellfleet the whale vanishes. The whale,
the woman, and the world—swallowed into their witnessing,

obliterated by being described. And now there are only words
in the mind and words are all that ever existed on that imaginary shore.

Look carefully and you can trace her prints across the sand:
inked footsteps disappear at the edge of the cruel water.

And now the current swells like a fever, and eternity, having stalked
its golden moment, rushes in—like the names of wildflowers

damned against the fingering mind, or the novels women wrote
too much like her own, like the images from early dreams

entering the gate, Zephyrus and Aura tumbling down a sky,
the broadcast seedscape of airway static, brocade embroidery

swimming up like starling swarms through the valleys, as in the folds
of Eleanora's dress or Uccello's lances bristling into the cries of waxwings

and a rain of ashberries on the faun-seeking satyr and sacred bull led
to sacrifice beyond the lovers' frozen kiss, relics drifting in on the river's

braided power where fleet overfall, the burnished splash of photographs'
mercury, translate into charging warhorses on the sea's floodtide.

And now the underside of thought ravels like the back of a tapestry
where adenine, thiamin, guanine and cytosine ladder up in knots

to undo your cells, orchids zipped open so pollen grains spill
from anthers of your words onto the sepal and axil of the mind

or the dotscape of impact craters mapped against the meteor's death
from the Quadrantids to the Leonids slung beyond the hammock's

declining crescent—memories, images, facts, solutions, pages, words
fusing in the scree slope in the wake of your delving, and selfhood pours

back through the channel—you count the breaths along the submerged
talus slope of the channel where the whale passed and time presses in.

O generous sojourn that must fade of its loveliness—
cut into memory and it is always green to the fuse!

The narrow end of eternity looks like a conch shell,
like the double helix of a whelk's egg case in dried seaweed,

like a Hartshorn and Sons bottle from Boston glazed with
the sand-wash translucency of tides. It looks like a beach

festooned with the husks of fiddler crabs' pincer claws
smiling in the sun. It looks like a book, the one written

by the woman at the table in front of the window where
the wide reach of time opens up in the form of the sea.

Like the story told to daughters of mermaid potions,
and skeleton pirates, and talking crows, or of being roped

to the piling as the tide rises and the stories self tells self
about the smell of air on the Sea of Cortez or on a bay on Waldron

Island, the itch of salt and sun on skin. And this is where
she has arrived, at the end of the crazy song,

at the beginning of the nameless where she will shed
story itself—*once upon a time there was this girl*—and step out of prophecy:

*the woman who imagined the Wellfleet whale will live on this island*
*within the year.* It feels like the pencil lodged between her fingers

and the doodled horse sketched on a legal pad's margin, like the arm's
muscle memory of returning the ping pong ball with enough topspin

to alter the trajectory of the planet toward Pleiades, like an unadorned
room, like sounds from the harbor drifting across the wall, light glancing

off Blackfish Creek and Drummer Cove to conform
with the current of sleep or waking without memory

into the pure hard now where the surf off Wellfleet
and all the driven things under the driven stars stir and rise.

# LEARNING TO BREATHE

Is it the meadow sloping down to the bluff
where thistle and harrow brush a horizon of orchard
grass and distant sea, where bent and dog's tail

sway above knapweed and a stem's spittle mass
opens to the tent a spider wove over the warren
path, decked with fur, where rabbits cut close

to the heather? Or is it wildrose adorned with mussel
shell, snakeskin and foxprint that tell you you've come
to the edge of things again? Eagles could tell us

about the rising tide by their study of seal flesh
but keep their own counsel. Shipworm burrows
are signs of the skiff freed by the rising water of summer's

fullnesses. Yes, seas rise and fall, and the encroachment of waters
sends you scrambling against the blackberries. Never mind—
paths will open up where imagination lights a need.

And as the seas rise wishes that sailed complete
their circumnavigations with their haul: moons, words,
winds, spices from far shores. And now with floodtide

you can hear minor gravity in the curl of the waves:
breathe in the music of gravel and shell, cockle and whelk
as they stir the shorebirds to sing warm times to the cold.

# AFTER SONG

It's only after, when my fingers radiate the ferrous
scent of the strings that the music reveals its fatedness,

how everything burns clear through, like pages held too close
to a hot light, the separation of this and this opens,

then flames, then opens again into a shadow of what it was.
It has been weeks since I touched the guitar, weeks since

the last false spring lifted from the snow-welded streets,
and now it's snowing again in late March. Song seems

uneasy in its cradle of zinc and bronze, but now it too has
called for hands to fret its gauges,

and like a ship hauling its anchor through the heavy brine
of the world, something surges with the tide to bloom

from a spruce rosette. Already the snow melts and sirens
wail through town, there's the moan of a train, and fingers

sting where steel tattooed inky indentations. Ribs
strain to begin again where the heart breaks open,

moments chasing each other to a finale, quilted measures,
the fade of flaring sparks, the diminished ringing of something

that just happened resolving into the retina's after-burn
of snow, oxidized metals sustaining the after of the song.

# CHIMFUNSHI

## i.

I see it in your eyes—
the woods are singing

and you are thinking of home.
I see the crazy sun

and the weight of the continent
on your back, miles endless

like the hours that have brought
us here. Where have we been,

you and I, that this is the place
where we are always arriving,

that this sky above the dambo
drains every spark from every thought

into the gathering place of eternity?
No matter, this is where we've come:

the arms of the masamba tree
above the fire

holding back night's heaviness
even as it falls to free us from our cares.

## ii.

And what are they, these cares for home,
noise from the other room, the smoke

of the map burning the language
of colonial rule on the buildings

telling us we too have history here
whether we've chosen to or not?

Our irritations bloom like the clouds
that open every day to taunt the farms

along the village road with rain
that never falls, not in this dry winter

we've come to know. But look again
at this village, study the life we can only

imagine: the weight of malarial water,
a child turning a stick and stone into a toy,

toil that is the only joy, love itself a viral
gamble, a loaf of bread wealth untold

among the orphans' relatives. Our troubles
are our own: practical luxuries of people

who have wandered from this native land
into the world of things with its own beauty

and its own time, its own burning map.

## iii.

The woods are singing in our eyes
and people rush to be born before they die.

Time is the wilderness in which we're lost,
time and desire brushfires at the edge

of the mind, snapping with the electricity our lives seek.
Yes, you and I have marked hidden paths

like that innocent road into Congo across the Kafue
whose perfect waters and perfect crocodiles

tell us though we may be here on this earth
we are never home, because we followed

a thought out of the trees and broke the long quiet
with our words. And now we live at the end of something,

you and I, and at the beginning, too. I see it
in your eyes—a path opening through dove feather

and acacia thorn. Let us follow it all the way into the hearts
we open to keep generous and wild as these singing trees.

# READING A POEM I DON'T UNDERSTAND

Some of what happens in the poem I don't understand
is perfectly clear, like the men falling through the floor

of their own desire, or the crickets whirring at the moon.
But how the hours mend these broken things with birds,

a book on a table, elbows, the pillow, instinct and dream,
the onomatopoeic *ric-ric* of the gears of the catastrophe,

or how the rain finally lifts them and drowns their flames
remains mysterious, like a story problem about cars

leaving different towns at different times and speeds
and meeting at an inscrutable roadside stop where the poem

gleams as a shrine for the knowledge that died there.
The women in the poem I don't understand are beautiful

and mysterious and indifferent and I think I'd like to know
them and wonder if I already do, but these have redefined

intimacy as the exchange of pebbles gathered by a river,
the one that runs near the road where the two cars meet,

and somewhere along that stretch of long miles they can be seen
selecting the stones where the world has delivered them

by measures that have the same indiscernible principles as
the problem told in the story. Somehow I missed it or missed out,

the aptitudes for distance failing like those for the near.
To mark my way here I've torn scraps from the poem

I don't understand and drop them along my trail
so I can find my way back to a simpler ignorance

before the birds and rain fuse the words
to the indecipherable landscape and the poem

begins further enchantments of another, obscurer desire.

# SEVENTEEN CAMELS

As far as the laws of mathematics refer to reality,
they are not certain; and as far as they are certain,
they do not refer to reality.

—*A. Einstein*

Maybe the father wished for his sons to miss him
when he was gone. When he heard death knocking,

the caravan stretched from his door through the desert,
and in its hope was the strength of his soul. He saw

maids gathered at the grinding stone and thought of his daughter's
malachite eyes. He gave his sons their legacy of seventeen camels:

to the eldest, half, to the middle, a third, to the youngest, a ninth.
When he died, the daughter wound a thorn from the field

through her hair and wept. The sons sat calculating in the yard,
sucked pebbles, and scratched the dust, baffled.

That's how the story's told. And in that story a stranger arrives
to do the math. But in the story that is not told,

what the father really wanted was for the sons to understand
the meaning of absence, which is the meaning of love.

And in the untold story it was the sister who carried water
from the well outside the village back to her father's house,

the sister who'd watched the donkey pick its way over the barren path
and graze where the grass still held dew. It was the sister who said,

Brothers, add my donkey to your legacy, imperfect though it be,
as our father would wish. Only remember me when your inheritance

is settled. And the brothers considered the eighteen, and the eldest
took half, nine camels, the middle a third, six camels, and the youngest

a ninth, two camels. The leaders of men set their caravan across the desert
for linen, brass, and wine as a sweeping rain threatened the harvest.

And the daughter led her remembrance,
the eighteenth, braying against the wilderness.

# QUEEN THIEDBERGE ESCAPES FROM TOUR DE LA REINE

The Queen's tower rises in the heart of the King.
She foresees the coming of Geneva and Savoy

like weather gathering to storm the castle.
She witnessed her husband's infidelities in the glow

from the hearth, in ribbons of glacial wash
intertwined like snakes. Prison is release

from the predatory eye of the King
who mints his zeal in his slaves' foundlings.

A tatter-winged crow drops from the turret
like a sycamore leaf. A nuthatch flies out

of the fireplace. From across the lake, Alps teach
the ice of her burning how to flame. Perhaps she'll go

there when she escapes her rage, to study how rock and snow
define the limits of things. The surprise is how terrible

endurance is without love. Love—a thimble's dream
of sea. The mortar of her coffinette crumbles

beneath the hoardings. Against her eyelid
machiolations impress the blueclad relief

of the sky. The face of the monk beside the hawk house
shines even at this distance. Soon he will show her the walls

at Talloires. Her stairs shine like moons recording the days
of her passing. Too, moonlight shines on the staircase

inside that other tower filled with water, the place
that describes the shape of the life she dares to live

inside her rage. From the stables signs the animals
scare at a fox or at others of the King's cruelties. Tournette

waits in the distance, inclining toward further heights.
Mouse slips from cat under the stone bench.

Lothaire's hawk perches on the fence of the sheepfold.
Bone-stairs lead from her tower into the waters of Annecy.

Now, for safe passage. The king wenches in the old dwelling.
Cur sniffs in corners. The fire spits.

From the forest, wolves howl the same hunger,
thoroughly human, into which the Queen descends.

# DRAWING

Winter fingers release
an inky river north.
In a paper sky smoke
curls, a primitive
cartoon sketched
where alphabet
birds rush the spiral
sun on. Listen.
This sun has the sound
of paper hushing
against itself,
as the river
sweeps out from
minimal mountains
crayoned on newsprint
where the child's drawing
prophesizes the edge
of everything as
the future unrolls
beyond reach
of a drawing hand.

# ALMA ROSÉ, VIOLINIST AT AUSCHWITZ

We'd like to think that taste burned out the tongue
that told them how to die, sweetness an acid wash
of memory remembering sweet, wine the weeping

of fruit bruised by a season passing, harvest of frost
after too much rain or too little, soil burned
or corroded by the lime of years. Words too, endearments

turned into misunderstanding, the distortions suspicion
slips into the jealous mind, fatigue baffling the best
intentions, we could wish for so much. And as rosin

dust from the violin lifts into the air of their
undreamed future, it may be necessary to believe
their ears had turned to stone, each note grinding

harder against the absence of joy they wore as delight
on the face of diversion, and what they heard were
memories of hearing, the pulse of blood which shared

the same hold on life as blood they shed, that dumb
void a measure of the emptiness they affirmed, sound
canceling sound, as life erases life. And that it lifted

the musicians out of misery, washed the terror and numb
exhaustion from them and wrapped the certain warmth
around their desolations until all they knew gathered

into an ecstasy of forgetting, redeemed in the tremor
of string, the undulations of the Danube, a butterfly
imagined clearly, loose above the dead yards. But it was never so.

For here there was a cruel justice in the consolations
of the orchestra, and as she ministered the air with her hands
even malevolence seemed a portion of the daily bread

and in this were enemies loved, and hurried downstream
to their despair, for beauty is the measure of all things, and works
the evil with the good, to break the fearful beating of our hearts.

# THE GATES OF PERUGIA

She drifts over landscape afterimages of stone
    grafted onto the hillsides of Umbria, shadows
over olive groves, the dust of human smoke

petrified into a scar. Why break a pastoral
    to wall in a field of stone? Must men flood
over men like the iron edge of will?

History is the adornment of landscape with blood,
    the invention of cockle and lily in symbolic flight
to fix a specific gravity in the walls of a city.

She is only a woman looking at the hills of Umbria.
    At the hotel there is a wolf the owners raised from a pup,
its fur tallow to the touch, its eyes a gray so empty the world

the woman sees completely fills it. She has stepped out
    of time and country to come to this place, as the wolf has moved
out of its wilderness into this particular bewilderment—

a chlorinated pool above the olive grove, a hearth and Persian
    carpet and eucalyptus spray fragrant in the table vase.
The wolf and the woman watch the city move in the mind.

A mind is not history, but a drift of wind over dust.
    Our oracles lead to the atrium where the limits
rise above themselves. She asks the city for what she wants,

for the nearness of body and heat, for the bustle
    of streets outside the window, for the larger thing of which
she is a part, the reach of family and story she may die

out of without fear that her dying ends it all. The town
    walls are her walls. What does safety in numbers mean
to these congregations of sin? Is it that a god needs

worshippers, or that wolves follow hunger down from high
          snows? People come from people, not from fields.
So walls are not the borders of nations but the weight

of what happens, maiden and knight in praise
          and fear of some god, a refinement of appetites
the keening sword carves at the edge of electrons.

She'd like that too, a blue knight to melt into her dream,
          the way a city is a being born to the contingency of bodies
under the shade of Monti Sibillini. Now there's

weather fixing above the gates of Perugia where a particular
          rain reads the faces of Corso Vannucci, where it
fingers names of certain families that told others

how to live. And that's where she fails a little again—
          that beauty comes from power, that when a field is broken
by stone people die. A city is not only the deposit wind invested

between its birth and death, an outpost of deities
          at the edge of a civilization's name, what's left
after rage delivers Umbrian soil down the Tiber

to grind against the empire's heart of flint. A city is the law
          of her nature, her own hungers legislated through decree.
The names of wars, Sienna and Arezzo, Spoleto and Assisi,

spilling from popes' brains like seed from sacks of grain,
          are names of their cities, of her foreign pleasures consumed
like market trinkets bought under the shield of griffin or lion.

Edicts, laws, names, canons, reforms—what are these
          but walls for keeping some things out and others in?
She reads that the onyx band marriage-ring of Mary

lies inside the chapel and wonders what it means
          that an Etruscan arch folded into a Roman gate
guards such relics across the street from walls

stenciled with unicorns and painted raw with graffiti.
          As she watches, a city in Umbria meets the mind with stone,
like the hard thing a soft thing moves through or over.

A hillside town carved in stone is the body the mind
          enters, the mind metaphorical in ways the body never is.
She watches from the eyes of a foreigner, from a place where a wolf

has become a dog, where the temple of Minerva
          has become a fresco in a rosary of sites on the grand tour.
To her the city is the mind, the mind she wants to recover

from the wars of men and the old women spinning
          revenge. In Palestine and Babylon a god is still worth
the purchase of blood, but here decadence reads like

the calm prose of a tour book. Somewhere in the city
          people are doing unspeakable things newspapers
have mapped out in headline ink so black it shines.

Ours is a belonging between nowhere and everywhere—
          her thoughts begin to wander home. Walls define the fields
as skin the body of our blood. Where wolves roam the margins,

fields remain unfixed in another kind of forever
          she will never know, outside the mind, where wind ranges
over the stony heights to the forest and mountains

above, though she's come to understand that at her end of history
          a wolf is the world's way of knowing itself unfettered,
of slipping past the gates to the fields beyond.

## THE UNARMORED CHARIOTEER DRIVES
## THROUGH THE EMPEROR'S DOMINIONS

Time has burnished the unarmored charioteer's
terracotta face to a black patina.

The unarmed charioteer steps from the grave
into the fragments of the emperor's broken life.

That history is a slender reed balanced on fingers
under a sky where stars are pendant fortunes,

the unarmored charioteer reads in the brittle ribs
chronicling the dynasty of leaves. Under the same

dominion, emperor and charioteer alike muse
from the mausoleum of days.

The unarmored charioteer holds out his hands
to grasp the harness of earth as it revolves.

Look—where chromium oxide inscribes
the fate of the cavalry, crumbling under the stars

of the workshop's ceiling! A warrior is a bronze
casting whose wax and plaster mold has burned

to a terracotta socket. Emperor Qin Shi Huang unites
the warring factions of fullness and emptiness

into an empire where a warrior is a clay soldier
carving roads and canals before the ramparts of darkness.

The unarmored charioteer steers toward the scholars
the emperor had buried to examine the mind of emptiness.

Soil etches the lacquer daylight spilled
on the emperor's mortality. The unarmored

charioteer drives the human image deep into the earth
beneath the emperor's watchtower. The cosmos

is a tomb where all are buried alive to the motions
of infantry marching against the motions of soil and quartz.

A horse is a bronze casting that once galloped through the emperor's
domains. Death excavates from its cave everything that moves:

emperor, charioteer, the horse that pulls them, the nothing that drives
them. It sorts its artifacts with terracotta fingers, terracotta hands.

Terracotta is the color of blood dried by sand
rubbing the everyday into eternity.

# IN TINTORETTO'S *CREATION OF THE ANIMALS*

birds lie across the sky the way they would
upon the ground after the hunt—inert, stretched

out for measure, deployed like the pattern of death
from which the living would be crafted,

and the fish their shadowy reflection breaking
the water's surface of a sea dusky with their cold

blood summoned, and the hares and amphibians,
the thirsty wolf and the turning deer, they all

have the rough and tousled look of things
just waking up from an eternity of sleep

where they have been buried a long time
in the loamy soil of God's imagination

before the fall into being, needing gravity
and the elements to smooth their hides

and mend their feathers, as if the memory
of the third day still tugged them toward the earth

even as their first morning, the fifth day,
stunned them with the emptiness of night—

the shock of consciousness so cold and soft, memory
became the always now of a world utterly without words.

# MEREDITH

I was still hunkered in the alphabetized desks
of fifth grade when you took us to see Zappa

ripping the heads off dolls. The stage was a blur
because no one had figured out I needed glasses yet.

We learn to disguise our blindnesses early. You were
a flame buried in the wound of a fat body, and we knew

even then as the boys you cared about so much,
we were the ones you thought you'd never have yourself

since certain cruelties are non-negotiable, since no
one seemed to care so much about you—well,

we build up vicarious joys this way too. Our mother,
like you, was dying even then, cladding her fire in the hard

shell disappointment layered up until the oxygen drained
away. It's hard to see through nacreous translucencies

when you're not trying. That pure part of you you gave
us when we weren't looking was distorted in the lenses of your

cat-eye frames, and now avidity looks like another form
of damage. But rain is nothing to a beach. I want there to be

a life lesson, some gem you gave me to refract the light
of now into prismatic understandings. But there's only you

and the earnest face through which you peered into mine.
Maybe you saw all of our futures when you braved up

to that bleak night, the wounds accumulating like hours
until you ate your death in pills. There's only so much

they'll tell a child. But when you died my mother faltered
and the part of her that wished to extinguish itself in gin

has been unreeling, with a will slower than yours, ever since.
Who could have known that we'd all still feel like children

forty years later, who would have thought that the only
way to enter life would be by dying? If necessity

is the mother of invention, what name do we give
unrecognized losses, the ones that take decades to catch

us? Yours will do, and I'll remember brave you this way,
Meredith, unfolding the disguises to find a way to care.

# ELEANORA

*In her recent exhumation, Eleanora of Toledo, Duchess of Florence from 1539–1562, was found to have been dressed carelessly after death.*

### i.

A Duchess dies into her portrait the way history
is born. Her body diminishes, bodice
and stockings loosen, the halls of the palazzo

recede like the memory of power or the folds
of the eleventh afterbirth the astrologer
secreted away. Each child pulls from the Duchess

a fist of chance through a banded sleeve;
failed embassies retreat through the halls of the Duke.
The Duchess dies into her clothing, each gold pearl

a star blown across her imagined life, and her real one,
made from hours of drowsy pain. A blouse unlaced
is the sound of voices from the silk market outside her rooms,

the corridor echoes with footsteps of the sculptor who stole
her bronzes now soldered to the sockets of the pedestal
where Perseus puzzles over Medusa's severed head.

It's always a duchess's actions bind consequence
like paint to the walls of daylight. The world grows thin
as a fresco, each room an interior of the mind's skull,

rendered in colors malarial, shapes grotesque. A duchess lives
to die through a chenille sleeve slipping against the wrist,
the sheen of embroidered velvet in guttering candleflame.

Memory shrinks within the cloth that marked the motions of grace.
There was a Spain once, a place her body knew and thoughts fingered
as forgetting. Swifts flicker above the piazza. A duchess dissolves

into the chambermaid's regret. A sculptor muses as bronze
hardens to the same fluid cast of the zimarra she wears.
A duke's words die over stone. A chambermaid's words

complete her lady's thoughts. The waiting woman threads
the clasp of the necklace in her dreams. Contagion smothers the Duchess
in taffeta. The Duchess drowns in filaments of gold and silver.

When a duchess dies calcium no longer leeches from her bones
each time she bears fruit of the Duke.
When a duchess dies she becomes the fruit

that bearing seed dies, the husk of wheat
planted in a tomb. She becomes the shadow of eleven moons
orbiting home, a crater off Naples where a burning star

extinguished another life. Pestilent air of Pisa drifts
from the river to the visitors' chambers, carries a woman
from this world where she is a stranger in a cage of bones.

## ii.

Eleanora, travelers walk the halls of your palazzo now.
We are the afterlife through which your memory moves,
an extravagance of history haunting corridors you sloughed

off, old skin of stone, for the new house on the hill
where the future rose over the ancient town like a wind
that smelled of sea air. From somewhere in this future you

died out of we opened your sarcophagus and invented
another story to tell about your bones, about the folds
of your uneasy repose, about the undoing of your portrait.

Maybe as we removed your clothes the varnished oils
of flesh pleated and ravaged grew a new burden
to weigh down your arms and legs,

to teach us how to die, how to dress for death.
Maybe your roots should have been given to richest loam,
maybe your skin should have been dismantled by soil

instead of snake-sloughed through marble's vacancy.
The madness of your children resolved into the fury
of our scholars' history, pain exfoliated as years.

Not even your painter could save you from certain
darknesses. Not even the wealth of kingdoms
stitched into your brocade dress. And the mother's

pomegranate that adorns your royal fabric
is cloth's bane bearing the six garnets Persephone
swallowed whole. Not all underworlds look like memory.

Some resemble the portrait of you that hangs in the corridors
of the offices the Duke commanded. Some look like
private halls buried beneath the old palazzo's crenellations,

like the road you took above the river where sycamores raised
brittle branches into the painter's light, the road that promised
a villa with a view of the sea and blue sunlight falling

all the way to Toledo. There's no way to dress for eternity,
you've shown us that. Hands always move the hurried blood
toward decay. Maybe the least strange thing is to die.


### iii.


To be in a room and then not, or to be in a room and then
become the room and whatever more, yes. And now,
Eleanora, we come down to it. You know what they say of how you

were dressed—that fear of infection led your ladies
to be careless, to skip eyelets in lacing your gown,
to put on a stocking inside out, one not even matching its mate,

to improperly hook your bodice and poorly compose the blouse
of gold pearls and disregard the silk and satin, velvet and taffeta,
drowning you in your zimarra a loose sheath your body now failed

to fit, like her mother's finest dress on a little girl fed on fantasy.
How many waiting ladies does it take to dress a duchess?
Isn't what they say about fate true also of attendants:

most present at birth, marriage, and death? They would have known
your clothes would outlast you, the days rubbing, molecule by molecule,
grains of your body into dust. And yes, mortality

is disease, the doomed background against which Bronzino's portrait
always flames. Maybe you were past words and knowing, maybe not.
Maybe I'm talking to myself, the way the Duke did in your room.

Maybe all of history is just a muttering as the walls burn,
stories we tell to shore up the hours.
The way the Duke did when he dismissed the women,

the way he did when he pulled the wreck of you
from that wasting sheet, when he unpinned his dumb heart
to gather the nothing there and feel the body fail to love him back,

then the raveling: bodice, blouse, stockings,
dress, the fabric that held you, the cloth that holds.
After, a Duke's is the work of stupid men handling the old

times as they change into the new. A duchess still is dying
into what words become when they cannot be the thing itself,
the materials our hands use to dress us with flames.

# ALCHEMIES

It is then to this world, *the world in which I find myself*
*and which is also my world-about-me,*
that the complex forms of my manifold
and shifting spontaneities of consciousness stand related . . .

—*Edmund Husserl*

### i.

Birds flock from San Marco
to decipher the sky as a form of pure knowing

whose sound is the shape of bells tolling from the campanile,
to read the sky as a depth we can only imagine

to be the thrill of gravity's push, a fall
into that uncertain rising above Florence.

Birds probe where the caesura of the window
configures the self as the world fleeing its desire,

as figures retreating into distance's infinite sadness,
into the red dark day simmering down to disappear.

The intimacies of images die into themselves
as the photographer opens the world to light's

scratching on the lens of the heart :
metaphor's palimpsest—bird, sky, color, mind,

heart, difference itself—figures, all figures,
euphoric, disphoric, the finger's whorl smudged

against that wound where the world and self merge,
the bird and the spiral gaze.

## ii.

In café Sant' Ambrogio confusion falls to a hum.
church bells die,

and the calcio ends zero to zero
but the sound track rises as the barista

shoots her colleague a venomous look
and the machine in the corner manufactures

the darkness that drives it all directly into the bloodstream
of the Arno. It's one of those mix tracks recycles an old blues

voice riffing like a verbal tick, and now
the music's in your own language and fails

as white noise, even with the synthesized gulls
crying over the back curl of the song. The square

blooms into evening people promenading
against a twelfth century wall.

From a child's bicycle the panhandling thug
squints through the swollen eye someone's fist

closed for him at the street he weaves down
like a circus bear on a trike and passes

the reeking man who lives in front of the post office
across from the Standa, a grocery cart a home

against the old towers rising above Lion's Fountain
where shadows have given us new words

to describe the world.

## iii.

Maybe this is the way beauty enters time—
as a nymph wrapped around wind,

wind, a Zephyr draped with a woman's limbs,
legs, tendrils of hair, or folds of mantel and wing

intertwined, the way all things in the mind
become one another. A sea drifts ageless blue

against a shore of trees sweeping the sky
with their seasons and the loveliness

of change. But our nakedness in birth tells
us how earth must be caught:

before the gilt pigments of the allegory
distract us to the surface once again

and make us forget that all truths are about the self
or about the terrible world.

Beyond the play of mass and line, where shape
colors laurels against imagination's canvas,

only human language can describe the divine.
Finally a goddess rises beyond the horizon of piety,

an unscorned Magdalene who will never know
the trials of having a perfect son. Let it go, let it go.

It is not possible to lie about the body or its pleasures,
any more than it is to defy the cloak time holds

to subdue her under the lacquered waves. And just so
voices claim the gallery and we enter into that other dream.

# IN THE HALL OF CLOCKS

The photographer's flash throws your shadow across
the display case, glass on glass, all densities

transparent against these aged faces, thin as a sheet of carbon
one atom deep, a thinness only the mind can hold

without being sliced into something less than itself,
less than you.

And then there's the you that eclipsed light that way,
a body adorned with the particularities

of dress and coat, layers of appearance shaping light's
current down to shoes' flayed pigments.

Our enumerations configure all turns of this maze,
corridors of the museum, decision and fatedness

that move you through your unique map of time,
all the while aslant a face light presses with alternatives to desire.

Desire is the way a mind predicts the future of the body
as coils of cells rubbing against other spirals.

Even your face wears in the filtered light, the same filtered light
glancing off dial and shoe. How can we measure what changes

as you tie a lace, beyond counting heartbeats? The dramas
of before and after settle in your mind as noise in the hall

arranged into discrete sounds—murmuring, pocketed coins,
hobnails scuffing marble floors. Like a musical phrase returning,

your face rises above the cabinets. Tides turn the way leaves do,
only daily. Is it the fraying scarf or coughing guard that lends this crimson

to the room? Earlier a waitress finger-drummed her impatience
at the cup's emptying before it cooled. Soles wear out, like skin,

a cloud's shade passes between embraces, between memories of decades
old kisses. Moons on your fingernails grow and fade, the worrying thought

of a solitary meal. Sounds from the hall tell you that in the end
there is only fate and its enduring, imagining ourselves into other lives.

They're all abstract now, the measures of that cooling cup, the cup's
emptying, turned pages, birdsong disappearing over the hill.

You can't see them, wheels inside wheels of the tiny wound engines
that can never beat like yours. Can you hear them tell you

you're a passing shadow, a musical phrase on the verge of hearing,
can you feel those lifeless hands around your heart?

## MORPHINE WATCHES THE SLEDDERS

A muted fury squeezes tonight into a fist of ice
releasing a peculiar warmth as ageless as the blue
twilight. December and the neighborhood
have conjured some kids at the top of the hill
and unaccountable moons bloom and dissolve
around their heads. Cobbles ache under snow
in the shape of the hill that has brought them
here outside my house on the corner.
If the sledders look up as if with one motion
what they sense is the wind that blows
all the way around and back again.
Their vanishing is a puzzle revealing
how only memory held them there, a watching
of remembered image playing out beyond
the thing itself. And then they're back, huffing
ice from their fingers, momentary presences
the darkness rifts open to pull them beyond
country, beyond where history meets the future
along the same parallel lines the runners leave in the snow.
From beneath the hill they tramp to the bonfire
gleaming down by the pond, also ageless in the blue
the mind navigates to follow them there.
Reeds die at the edge of the water like threads
from a frayed cuff where its black sleeve of silvery
acceptance bleeds to make possible the world.
Taking hold again, the itch inside my skin, pure thistle
in the blood, makes everything glow an amber light:
the table's hardwood, the bead of gold in the tumbler,
the lazy crenellations where the pie's crust
is unbroken, its smashed fruit. What amazes
is how time swallows pain down this way
through deep fissures the opiates have levered open.
And now the pull of the familiar, the burn in the throat,
a flicker of appetite shifting through the body's tectonics,
how the glass and fork and pie tin configure

the rightness of things. At the window it's all blue
and silver again as the hour performs its hocus pocus
on anguish and joy. Absence unfolds its layered self until—
there they are, the sledders again, morphine blowing hot
the dark coals of their faces swimming up the pane glass,
blossoming like the world's own bourbon ache:
yes, here, now, the emptiness gives way.

# REMEMBERING

*for Glen*

Close your eyes and begin to count,
and confess you don't know how beauty is born

again into the world. Reach out to touch its golden
skin with those same lips salt seared when winter

dropped the dumb stone of death into your hand.
Tell yourself you couldn't give life reason

to live, but behind the leaves of your tale
find the final nakedness beyond words,

where the thing lets us go. Remember that silver
hillside that sheds us like rain?

That's what love is up against, beyond the mind's
grasp and time's rinsing, there on the hill

where birdsong sounds like happiness. Now tell
yourself it's about to rain, and lift your face and hands.

Build your grief at the bottom of the valley
where the floodplain gathers all our darknesses

to draw them out. Go and stain this Kentucky dirt
with bourbon piss, breathe in the smoke of your dying

and damn the strengths that keep you here. Enough is enough—
too, those damned birds and their enchantments.

Stop counting and take your hands from your eyes,
and call her at the top of your lungs: *All ye all ye in come free.*

## EGG

Surface tension is an art in the breaking house,
rubble held together by veneers of dust, moss,

flaking paint, palomino patterns of disintegrating
linoleum. The woman in the house says this can't be

happening, and if she's talking about change
she may be right: each crack is a battle and treaty

business. Webs like lace banners of hopelessness
drape the mausoleum of other hopes whose

remains we don't bother to put underground.
Heat swarms the packed shelves and cupboards,

swoons in the kitchen where from plates and spoons
it serves up its mortal incubation. Words too possess

the languor of fish failing in a bowl of water, rising
and falling like seasons the flesh has forgotten.

Inside the bodies inside the breaking house
grains of bone and shell slip off and float like snow.

On the other side of the city as we talk about the surgery
the blue macaw is restless, Groucho-walking the limb

of its indoor tree and muttering beyond our discernment
self-evident truths in the form of guttural aphorisms.

And then, even though it really isn't so, it seems as if
all the flakes off our spines and all the bodies in all the rooms

are never finally lost but sifted into a clay bowl fired
by light and time into porcelain, the pressure

of the universe bearing down on this kiln of clay
and feather, of linen and concrete and chemical and hope:

put in a stone and take out shattered silk, put in cloud
and take out schist, put in crumbling bone

and from the nest of dishtowel and newspaper
beneath the hunched parrot, take out an egg.

# THE SMALLER CUP

We know things by their absence, warmth
by absence, love. We understand openings

by closing them, as with your eyes smoothing
the distances. We remember by shuttling images

along a wick, the machine of stars running
blood along a finger's touch. We measure

fullness by a bowl's brimming, time by
dust gathering on the face of a watch,

distance by how helpless words become.
And then it's as if the world sheds its clothing

and it is no longer October or November,
just some remote cast off planet turning

its engine over and over in some corner
of particularity where we find ourselves

at the end of something
as cold spills through the window
into a small bright cup.